# ANIMAL LI...

# DOLPHINS

## and PORPOISES

Sally Morgan

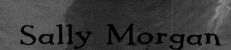

Picture credits
(t=top, b=bottom, l=left, r=right, c=centre, FC=front cover, BC=back cover)

**Corbis** FC - © Stephen Frink, 16cr © Hiroya Minakuchi/Minden Pictures
**Ecoscene** 17tl Phillip Colla.
**FLPA** 5tr Hans Leijnse/FN/Minden, 18-19 Flip Nicklin/Minden Pictures, 21bl Terry Whittaker.
**Getty Images** 1 UIG via Getty Images, 2-3 Panoramic Images, 4br UIG via Getty Images, 6bl Kevin Schafer, 6-7 Ai
Angel Gentel, 8bl Greg Boreham (TrekLightly), 8-9 Stuart Westmorland, 10-11 Jeff Rotman, 11tl Eco/UIG, 11br
Nature/UIG, 12bl UIG via Getty Images, 12-13 Tom Brakefield, 13tr Jim Borrowman, 14cl Alexander Safonov,
16-17 Justin Hart Marine Life Photography and Art, 18cl Pete Atkinson, 19tl James R.D. Scott, 22cl Reinhard
Dirscherl, 22-23 UIG via Getty Images, 23tl Jonathan Bird, 24bl Flip Nicklin, 24-25 Norbert Wu, 25br Timothy
Allen, 26bl Joanna McCarthy, 26-27 Eco/UIG, 27br Fco. Javier GutiÃ©rrez, 28bl
Stockbyte, 28-29 Stephen Frink, 30t Eco/UIG, 30c Eco/UIG, 31 Martin Ruegner.
**Shutterstock** BC(left) Natali Glado, BC (right) BlueMoonStore, 4-5 niall
dunne, 9tr BlueRingMedia, 14-15 pierre_j, 15tr BarryTuck, 20-21
(background) kanate, 20-21 (foreground) Kristian Sekulic, 21tr
anyamuse, 30b Ricardo Canino, 32 Willyam Bradberry.
**Other** 7br A Vampire Tear.

# Contents

# Dolphins
## and porpoises

Dolphins and porpoises are intelligent animals that live in the world's seas and rivers. They belong to a group of animals called **cetaceans**, which includes whales. Unlike fish, they have to come to the surface of the water to breathe.

## Bulls, sows and calves

A female porpoise or dolphin (far right) is called a sow, and her young (right) is a calf. The male is a bull.

## Pods

Dolphins and porpoises live in groups called pods. These can be very large.

Even large dolphins like to leap out of the water when they swim close to the surface.

## Marine mammals

Dolphins and porpoises are **mammals**. This means that the females give birth to live young and feed them milk. Unlike most other mammals, dolphins and porpoises do not have body hair. Their skin is sleek, smooth and rubbery to touch, and they have flippers instead of legs.

FANTASTIC FACT

Large bottlenose dolphins can grow to be 3.6 metres long, while the much smaller Hector's dolphin measures just 1.2 metres long.

# Dolphin
## and porpoise types

There are 37 types, or species, of dolphin and six types of porpoise. All porpoises live in the sea, while five species of dolphin live in rivers.

### River dolphins

River dolphins are often quite small. Some are just 0.9 metres long. They have a long, slender beak and a bulging forehead. Unlike other dolphins, they also have a neck.

## FANTASTIC FACT

Killer whales, false killer whales, melon-headed whales and pilot whales are members of the dolphin family. They are only called 'whales' because of their large size.

The small spinner dolphin lives mainly in tropical waters.

## Dolphin or porpoise?

Dolphins have sharp, cone-shaped teeth and long beaks, while porpoises have spade-shaped teeth and short, blunt snouts.

# Where they live

Dolphins and porpoises live in all of the world's oceans and seas, even in the very cold waters of the Arctic. Some are found all around the world. Others are only found in certain oceans and rivers.

The Pacific white-sided dolphin lives only in the Pacific Ocean.

## Shallow or deep?

Some dolphins and porpoises like to stay close to land in shallow water. Others, such as this rare Risso's dolphin, prefer to live in deep water.

Area where ocean dolphins are found.

The blue dots show where river dolphins live.

**FANTASTIC FACT**

Finless porpoises have fins on their sides but not on their back. About half of all the finless porpoises in the world have pink eyes!

# Giving birth

After a bull and sow dolphin have come together to mate, the sow will be **pregnant** for one year. She then gives birth to her calf.

## FANTASTIC FACT

The Indus River dolphin sometimes carries its young on its back, above the surface of the water.

## Being born

Dolphin calves are born tail first in the water. A newly born bottlenose dolphin calf weighs between 7 and 9 kilograms. The hungry calf feeds on its mother's milk, and grows quickly.

## Newborn calf

Soon after the birth, the sow pushes her calf to the surface so that it can take its first breath. As dolphins breathe through a **blowhole** on the top of their head, the newborn calf has to learn when to open and close its blowhole to avoid breathing water.

## First month

During the first month, the calf stays close to its mother. Her movements in the water help to pull the calf gently along.

# Growing Up

The young calf feeds on its mother's milk for about one year after it is born. When it is three months old, however, the calf's first teeth appear and it starts to eat fish as well.

## Playing

Dolphin calves spend a lot of time playing with their mother and with other calves in the pod.

## Having fun!

Dolphins enjoy racing through the water ahead of boats. They dart about the waves created by boats and leap out of the surf.

By playing together, young dolphins learn how to communicate with each other and how to hunt for food.

### FANTASTIC FACT

Adult dolphins sometimes show younger dolphins how to put bits of sponge on their beak for protection while hunting for food on the rough sea floor.

# Living in pods

Most pods contain about ten dolphins or porpoises, but sometimes pods join together to form large hunting herds. The biggest pods can have many thousands of animals in them.

## Hunting together

When out hunting, a pod communicates by whistling. If a mother joins a hunting group, her calves are often looked after by other sows in the pod.

*A typical pod is made up of mothers, calves and a few bulls.*

## Surfing

Dolphin pods love to go surfing on big waves, just like people do! Before the wave crashes, the dolphins turn around and head back out to sea.

## FANTASTIC FACT

A dolphin's main enemies are sharks and orcas, or killer whales. When under attack, members of a pod work together to chase off a **predator**.

## Leaving the pod

A calf is cared for by its mother for two years, or sometimes longer. After this, a female calf usually stays in her mother's pod, while a male calf joins another pod.

# A life in water

Dolphins and porpoises spend their whole life in water, rising to the surface to breathe. They usually come to the surface every two minutes or so.

## Keeping warm

Dolphins and porpoises have a thick layer of fat, called blubber, under their skin. This traps heat in their body and keeps them warm in cold ocean waters.

### FANTASTIC FACT

The deepest dive recorded for a bottlenose dolphin is 300 metres. This was made by a dolphin named Tuffy, who was trained by the United States Navy.

# Blowhole

When dolphins surface, they open the blowhole on their head and let out the air in their lungs. This blows away any water in their blowhole with a spurt, so that when they breathe in again, no water gets into their lungs.

A dolphin's blowhole is on the top of its head, behind its bulging forehead.

# Swimming

The dolphin's torpedo-shaped body is perfect for swimming. Its smooth surface allows it to move easily through the water at high speeds.

## Fast movers

Swimming at top speed, spinner dolphins can cover 10 metres per second.

↑ A spinner dolphin spins its body around as it jumps through the air.

## Tail and flippers

The dolphin uses its powerful tail to push itself forwards, and its two flippers to steer and brake.

Remora, or suckerfish

## FANTASTIC FACT

The fastest porpoise in the world is Dall's porpoise. It can reach a top speed of about 56 kilometres an hour!

## Spinning through the air

Most dolphins and porpoises enjoy hurling themselves out of the water and leaping in the air. The spinner dolphin, in particular, is a spectacular acrobat. It can leap and spin seven times in the air before entering the water again. Some scientists think spinner dolphins do this to shake off fish called remoras, or suckerfish, that stick to their skin.

# Feeding

Dolphins and porpoises are **carnivores**, or meat eaters. They eat a wide variety of fish, such as anchovies, mackerel, herring and cod, as well as squid.

## FANTASTIC FACT

Sometimes bottlenose dolphins will flip a fish out of the water with their tail flukes, and then eat the stunned **prey**.

## Swallowed whole

Dolphins and porpoises have small, sharp teeth, which they use to grip a fish's slippery body. They cannot chew so they swallow small fish whole.

## Dolphin teeth

Dolphins have as many as 90 small, cone-shaped teeth.

Dolphins swallow fish head first to prevent the spines on the fish's back from sticking in their throat.

## Big eater!

A bottlenose dolphin eats 20 kilograms of fish a day. This is the weight of 12 chickens! If a fish is too large to swallow whole, the dolphin may shake it until chunks break off.

# Senses

Dolphins and porpoises use their senses to find their way around and catch prey. They do not have a sense of smell, but their ears, which are inside their **skull**, give them excellent hearing. Most species also have good eyesight.

## Whistles and clicks

A dolphin uses its **melon** to produce whistles and clicks. The melon is found in its bulging forehead. It uses the sounds to communicate with other dolphins, as well as for **echolocation**.

## Listening to echoes

The sounds that a dolphin makes pass through the water and bounce off things to make the echoes that the dolphin uses for echolocation. By listening to these echoes, a dolphin can work out exactly where things are.

# Echolocation

This Atlantic spotted dolphin is using echolocation to find food on the sea bed.

Dolphins leave a trail of bubbles when they whistle.

# Hunting

Dolphins and porpoises use echolocation to find their fish prey. When they find a **shoal** of fish, they surround it. Then one or two members of the pod swim through the middle to catch the fish.

This shoal of fish has been split by a dolphin swimming through the middle.

## Shallow water

Some dolphins chase fish up onto mud banks, where the fish cannot escape. The dolphins eat the fish and then slide or flip themselves safely back into the water.

## Helping fishermen

In a town in Brazil, dolphins help the fishermen to catch fish. The fishermen stand on the shore with their nets in the shallow waters while the dolphins drive the fish into their nets.

### FANTASTIC FACT

The Ganges River dolphin from India swims on its side and drags a flipper along the riverbed to find any small animals hiding in the mud.

# Communication

Dolphins and porpoises make many sounds to communicate, including squeaks, grunts, trills and moans.

## Own sounds

Scientists believe each dolphin has its own type of whistle sound, and that many dolphins can recognise each other by the sounds they make.

## Chatty

Dolphins call to each other all the time. Their sounds travel quickly through the water, sometimes over long distances.

Dolphins and porpoises also communicate by touching and head-butting each other.

## Tail slapping

Dolphins sometimes slap the surface of the water with their tail. They do this to signal their annoyance, or to warn other dolphins of danger.

# Under threat

Dolphins and porpoises, especially river dolphins, are under threat. Each year, thousands die in fishing nets. Some dolphins even die from lack of food because people have taken too many fish from the sea. Pollution from chemicals and sewage also harms many dolphins and porpoises.

Dolphin-watching trips are popular with tourists in many parts of the world.

## Trapped

This striped dolphin is struggling to escape from a fishing boat's drift net.

# Helping dolphins and porpoises

Many organisations, such as the Whale and Dolphin Conservation Society, are working to safeguard dolphins and porpoises. More and more marine nature reserves now also exist where dolphins and porpoises are protected from hunting and fishing. Many fishermen now use special nets that do not trap dolphins and porpoises.

**FANTASTIC FACT**

The vaquita is the rarest porpoise. It is thought there are only 200 still alive. They are found in the Gulf of California.

# Life cycle of a dolphin

A female dolphin is ready to breed when she is four to eight years old. She is pregnant for one year and gives birth to a single calf. She may have a calf every two to four years. The smaller dolphins and porpoises do not live as long as the larger ones.

young calf with adult

older calf with adult

adult

# Glossary

**blowhole** the hole in the top of the head of a dolphin, porpoise or whale that is used for breathing

**carnivore** an animal that eats meat

**cetacean** a group of marine mammals that includes whales, dolphins and porpoises

**echolocation** a special ability to "see" using sound

**mammal** an animal that gives birth to live young, rather than laying eggs. Female mammals produce milk to feed their young

**melon** a structure in the forehead of a dolphin or porpoise, used for echolocation

**predator** an animal that hunts other animals

**pregnant** describes a female animal that has a baby, or babies, developing inside her

**prey** an animal that is hunted by other animals

**shoal** a group of fish

**skull** bones in the head that protect the brain

# Index